10K Titan: Push Beyond the 5k in 6 Weeks or Less!

by Scott O. Morton

© 2017 by LERK Publishing, LLC. All rights reserved.

LERK Publishing, LLC

Cover design: LERK Publishing, LLC

ISBN 978-1-947010-14-7

Follow me on Facebook and Twitter:

Twitter: @BeginR2FinishR

Facebook: facebook.com/BeginnerToFinisher/

Website: www.halfmarathonforbeginners.com

Email: scottmorton@halfmarathonforbeginners.com

To my dog, Halo.

Medical Disclaimer

The information in this book is meant to supplement, not replace, proper half marathon training. A sport involving speed, equipment, balance and environmental factors, and running, will involve some inherent risk. The authors and publisher advise readers to take full responsibility for their safety and know their limits. Before practicing the skills described in this book, be sure that your equipment is well maintained, and do not take risks beyond your level of experience, aptitude, training, and comfort level.

If you would like to know when I publish my new Ebook releases, please sign up by clicking here. All books can be read for **FREE** with Kindle Unlimited.

Beginner to Finisher Series:

<u>Available Now:</u>

Book 1: *Why New Runners Fail: 26 Ultimate Tips You Should Know Before You Start Running!*

Book 2: *5K Fury: 10 Proven Steps to Get You to the Finish Line in 9 weeks or less!*

Book 3: *10K Titan: Push Beyond the 5K in 6 Weeks or Less!*

Book 4: *Beginner's Guide to Half Marathons: A Simple Step-By-Step Solution to Get You to the Finish Line in 12 Weeks!*

<u>Coming Soon:</u>

Book 5: *Marathon Motivator: A Simple Step-By-Step Solution to get you to the Finish line in 20 Weeks!*

Why I Wrote This Book

I wrote this book for anyone push beyond the 5K. The 5K, commonly known as the gateway race, is by far the most the most popular running race. The 10K, is the next step in the running race chain, which will push your running capabilities. If you follow the training and steps outlined in this book, you will achieve this goal. This book is not intended to be a guide for the experienced runner. Increasing your speed and decreasing your finish times are not covered in this book.

Injuries & Medical Conditions

If you have sports related injuries, I highly suggest that you talk to a medical professional to determine if you are fit enough to endure running. Not seeking medical advice could further exacerbate an existing injury. I am not a legal or medical professional, nor am I offering any type of legal or medical advice. One last time, if you're injured or have medical conditions that prevent you from taking on a rigorous running training program, please seek the opinion of a licensed physician before participating in any physical training. While the training required for a half marathon is not nearly as difficult as the training for a full marathon, it will still push both your mental and physical capabilities.

What's in This Book

10K Titan will cover the bare bone basics of what is required to complete a 10K. This book will not cover any advanced running techniques. Its target audience is for beginner runners who want to push past the challenge of their first 10K. This book will introduce the topic of a long duration run. Some people classify a long run as any distance beyond the 5-mile marker. For the sake of this book a long run will be defined as any distance above and beyond your previous week's longest run. So, if the furthest distance you have run prior to starting a 10K training plan is 3.1 miles then anything greater than 3.1 miles will be considered a long run.

Some of the information within this book is repetitive. Some excerpts and information has been taken from my second book in the series, *5k Fury*. I wanted the reader to only have to purchase one book in order to finish a particular race. Please feel free to skip over the sections you may have previously encountered in my other books.

Assumptions

Before you dive into this book, I'm assuming the following:

- You can walk or run the distance of a 5K (3.1 miles).
- You will stick to a training schedule that is provided in this book or elsewhere.

If you are having trouble completing a 5k, I suggest following an easy paced training program to get you prepared for running a 5K. *5K Fury,* book number 2 in the series, Beginner to Finisher, will guide you through a step-by-step approach using a run/walk technique. The 5K training takes up to nine weeks and can be finished sooner depending on how physically fit you are. This is FREE to read with Kindle Unlimited. After you've completed the training for a 5K, you can transition into the six-week *10K Titan* training schedule.

—>   **Click here to read 5K Fury**   <—

If you're asking yourself, "Can I complete a 10K by only walking?" The answer is "yes." You can go as far as walking a half marathon if you select the correct course. A marathon is the one race that more than likely you will not finish within the time constraints by merely walking.

Chapter 1
Fear of Running Far

Fear of running more than a 5K

New runners fear running past the distance of a 5K (3.1 miles). Why do we fear running longer distances? Here is a list of some of the reasons we might tell ourselves as to why we don't attempt to run past 3.1 miles:

- I'm not a runner.
- I'm not a long distance runner.
- I fear that my body might not make it.
- I fear I might get injured.
- There is noway I can run that far and for that long.
- I can't run that far.
- I'm too overweight.
- I'm too out of shape.
- I'm too old.
- People might make fun of me if I tell them I'm training for a 10K.

The list goes well beyond some of the reasons listed above as to why we might be holding ourself back from running the distance of a 10K. There are too many "I can't"'s above. You have to shake loose the phrase, "I can't." That phrase poisons your mind with disbelief even before you get started.

Set the Training Start Date

Beyond the fear of running a 10K, another reason why runners don't complete a 10K would be not selecting a race date. Without a race date, you haven't created a running goal to shoot for and keep you accountable to train adequately for the race. It's not enough to just select a race date, you need to sign up for the race and click submit. Most races don't offer your money back unless you take insurance on your race purchases. Even buying insurance on your race day events, doesn't automatically get your money back. You still must qualify the reason why you missed the event. Medical related issues, a death in the family, are considered qualifying reasons due to medical visits.

After you select your race date, tell the world about your goal to finish a 10K. Tell your running partner, if you have one, and most importantly tell yourself. Write the goal down. Send yourself an email. Schedule a text message to yourself congratulating you on starting the training program. Once you have determined your race date, you need to work backward to determine when your start date for your 10K training should begin.

For example, if your 10K race were on Saturday, October 14th, 2017, then you would count backward six weeks which would place your start week on, Monday, September 4th,

2017.

Selecting Your Race

Choosing a favorable season as well as selecting a flat course will increase your overall race experience. In Texas, the spring and fall are great times to run. California is an ideal location to train and race due to the year-round fair weather. Many other states are good places to run as well. For a first-time runner, I want you to have a positive race experience. I don't recommend your first 10K to be in an environment that the temperature is greater than 80 degrees. Excessive heat will slow you down and increase your overall finish time.

For a list of 10K or 15K races, please visit the website Running in the USA.

Action Steps

- Purge the "I cant's" from your head.
- Select your race date.
- Sign-up for your race.
- Determine the start date for your new training schedule.

Chapter 2

Prepare Thyself for Running

Runner's Mindset

Getting past the fear of running is one of the biggest hurdles of completing any running race. I'm going to let you in on a big secret that helped me get past my fear of having to run. The secret is you don't have to run the entire race. Wow, what a secret. It's true. There will be many participants in a 10K that will run the entire race and not stop for water. If this is your goal, great! If you just want to cross the finish line regardless of walking or running or a combination of both, that works too! Once I realized that you don't have to run the entire distance, the fear of running vanished, instantly. My mind had found a weakness in the armor. I'm by no means a super athlete, just an average person with high beliefs that I could run. I hope that this encourages you to finish your first 10K no matter what age you begin at. If I can do it, so can you.

For a small pool of runners, finishing a 5K or a 10K can be accomplished with little or no training at all. This depends greatly on your age, health, and fitness level. For most new runners, following a training plan will get you to your goal faster and injury free better than simply winging it. Shield yourself from remarks such as, "you really can't say you finished a 10K if you don't run it." Nonsense! Put on your bullet proof, remark ricocheting armor and forge onward. You are running to train your body to complete your first 10K.

Many things that I go over in this book are solely my opinion. Every training schedule discussed within this book has been used by me at one point in my running career beginning with 5Ks through a marathon. There are several different schools of thought when it comes to how much running per week it takes to train for each race. There are different nutrition guides, shoe strategies, running miles per week, etc. When it comes to training schedules, there isn't a one size fits all schedule. Some things work better for other people, and some things will work better for you. There is, however, one common thing agreed upon by almost all runners - you have to believe in yourself and believe that you are a runner. Without this firmly ingrained in your head, you are exposing yourself to your minds ability to defeat your willpower. By telling yourself that you're a runner, it's almost as if you are giving your mind the permission to tell your body that you are a runner which in turn releases built up tension surrounding the idea that you're a runner. I'm not telling you this to discourage you. I'm telling you this to prepare you for the mental battle of running. Will there be days that your mind will sneak up on you and attack your running motivation? Of course, there will be. Telling yourself that you're a runner, however, will help minimize these mind sneak attacks. One week at a time, one day at a time, one mile at a time, and one step at a time will get you to the finish line.

The Power of Affirmations

When I trained for my first 10k race I had no prior knowledge of affirmations. Affirmations are positive action phrases you repeat to yourself on a daily basis to brainwash your mind. I made a list of affirmations that I repeated daily while training for races. Every time before I ran I would tell myself these affirmations:

- I'm a runner.
- I'm training for a 10K.
- I'm going to complete my 10K training.
- I'm going to cross the 10K finish line.

After I finished a long run, I would take the affirmations one step further and lie on the ground and concentrate on breathing. I would then visualize myself crossing the 10K finish line.

I contributed most of my success to believing in myself and knowing that failure wasn't an option. By repeating daily affirmations, you can trick your mind into accomplishing almost anything. Affirmations might seem a bit childish. However, they work if you are true to yourself and your level of commitment. Affirmations can be anything that you want them to be, old childhood dreams, new experiences, etc. The power is in the affirmation and hearing yourself say them. Give them a try for a week and see what happens.

Take a moment and write down a list of at least five affirmations. Title the list "Running Affirmations." Refer to this list every day, especially right before you go on a run.

Motivation

Why do some people finish marathons and other don't? I believe it comes down to self-motivation and determination. Self-motivation, while probably the strongest of any other form of motivation, is not the only source of motivation. There are several different types of motivation. Three types of motivation that I believe are the most influential come from social media, running partners and yourself.

Social Media

Social media can help keep you focused and motivated by your circle of friends. You can post running times and screen shots of your runs to social media to let your circle of friends comment and cheer you on. Social media will help perk you up when you have a day that you just don't feel like running.

Running Partners

Running partners are the next best thing to yourself keeping you motivated. They train with you. They give you feedback. They help you stay on pace. They push you when you have no more energy. Partners also help you stay accountable for following through with your goal. One caveat to a running partner is that if they lack self-motivation, they aren't going to be of much help motivating you.

Yourself

Self-motivation is by far the most powerful source of motivation. You know yourself better than anyone else. You are custom to knowing how your mind and body work. If you don't feel like running one day, tell yourself that you will just run a half a mile. After you run a half mile, tell yourself that you will just run one mile. By pushing yourself just a little bit, you can trick your mind into running.

Your motivation could be to get healthy and fit. Also, you could be motivated just to prove to yourself that you can finish a 10K or to donate to a worthy cause. Whatever the motivation is, you and only you will finish the race.

Action Steps

- Create your affirmations.

- Repeat your affirmations daily and before each run.

Chapter 3

Gather Needed Running Gear

Shoes

Don't skimp out on your shoes, especially if you are planning on running the entire 10K distance. I would invest some money in at least one good pair of running socks and running shoes. Some of the best brands of shoes for running include:

Adidas

Asics

Brooks

Nike

Mizuno

Saucony

Pronation

Depending on what your pronation is, you will need either a shoe that is built for flexibility, stabilization, or comfort. To determine which pronation you exhibit, you can use the wet feet on concrete test. Simply dip your feet in water and run a few quick strides across the concrete. Take a picture or just study your foot mark.

Entire foot showing - over - motion-control (flat feet)

Normal foot showing - normal - stability shoes (average)

Arch barely visible - under - cushioned shoes (high arch)

Pronation becomes more important when you start to routinely run much longer distances such as 4 miles and beyond. With each additional mile you insert into your weekly long duration run, the more stress you will place on your feet and legs. <u>Having adequate running shoes becomes a must at this stage of your running career.</u>

Running shoes have mileage and need to be replaced every 300 to 400 miles. I typically go through about 3 pairs of running shoes a year. Another way to extend the life of your shoes is to buy two pairs at once and alternate between each pair of shoes for each running session. My Garmin Connect application on my phone syncs with my Garmin Vivoactive Watch and tracks the mileage I place on my shoes. I can go visually see how many miles are on my current pair of running shoes at any time.

Clothing

Your shorts and shirt should be relatively loose fitting. If it's hot, you might prefer to wear a tank top to keep you cool on your runs. If it's cold outside, you should dress for the weather accordingly. However, even when it's cold outside, after your body has warmed up, you will want to start shedding clothes. If you are hot natured, which I am, the best thing to do on cold running days is to run in a circuit or loopback. If you run in a circuit, you can ditch your clothes after warming up and come back by on the same route and pick them up.

Socks

Find a good pair of socks that won't cause blisters. Balega socks are notoriously known for preventing blisters. They are a little expensive, but in my opinion, they are worth every penny. Balega socks are ultra-light by design, and you don't even notice that the sock is on your foot most of the time.

Some runners will prefer compression socks. Studies have shown that runners that wear compression socks tend to have less cramping and better endurance. The only caveat is that compression socks only help marginally until you get into the long distance running of 5 miles plus. Compression socks cover most of the calf and normally sit right underneath the knee cap. Either type of sock will do, but in my opinion, for a 10K, neither is better than the other, so it comes down to personal preference.

Wearables

Running with your smart phone is an ideal choice for many runners. On a smart phone, you can listen to music and track your run time and pace. There are hundreds of running apps you can install on your phone to do this. Couch 2 10K is probably one of the more popular running apps for 10Ks. If you do choose to run with a smart phone, I would buy an armband case that can be strapped to your fore arm or upper arm. If you want to hold your phone in your hands, I would alternate hands during your runs every mile or every 5 minutes. If you continuously use the same hand to hold your phone while you run, you are opening yourself up to improper balance injuries because of the added weight during your gait cycle. Your gait cycle is the locomotion that your legs and body make to complete one leg stride from lift off to touch down.

Apple 2 sports watches, Garmin VivoActive watches, and Fitbits are alternatives to bringing your phone along for a run. One drawback is that you don't have a phone in case of an emergency and the other is that you don't have music to listen to. One fix is to buy a small MP3 player such as a Clip-on Sandisk Sports MP3 Player and load it up with MP3s. I currently run with Garmin VivoActive HR and a Sandisk MP3 player. I don't like the extra bulk and weight of a smart phone. Again, this comes down to preference and what kind of wearables you want to dawn.

Other

When I run, I have to wear sunglasses. Sunglasses do the obvious by helping reduce the sun in your eyes. However, I find they serve a second equal purpose. Sunglasses help block the wind in your eyes. On a windy day, you will beg for sunglasses to help prevent your eyes from tearing up when you run.

I sweat a lot when I run, so I have to wear a headband. Females that have long hair will probably want to tie back their hair when they run.

Most importantly don't forget your sunblock.

Action Steps

- Buy good running socks (Balega is a great brand).

- Buy good running shoes.

- Use an app or wearable to track your run time and pace.

Chapter 4

Proper Running Posture

Tension is Thy Runner's Enemy

Body tension is your enemy. When your body is tense, you are spending extra energy because your body is having to hold your muscles in that flexed position. Try relaxing your shoulders and concentrate on breathing for a couple of cycles. This will normally ease tension in the body within seconds.

Foot Strikes

Your feet need to move in short quick steps and land underneath your hips. Your feet shouldn't land out in front of your hips.

Many different studies have tried to give scientific evidence over where you should land on your foot while running. There are three different locations on the feet where impact is made. The Forefoot, Mid-foot, and Heel. If you ever take the time to research the topic on foot striking, you will see just how conflicting reports are on the subject. In my opinion, I believe there is no difference on where your foot should land. The ideal location for your foot to land is the mid-foot. Heel strikers have a slightly higher tendency to over-stride, which is not good. If you start to become extremely sore or running becomes extremely painful in areas of your feet, you will want to get your running gait cycle analyzed by a running store.

Arms

Most runners don't think of their hand placement during a run. Your arms should sway back and forth naturally without tightening up your fists and pulling them in close to the body. The arms should never reach beyond 90 degrees on the upswing in front of your body. For best practice, your arms shouldn't rise above your belly button on the upswing.

Head

Try to keep your head lifted up. You will be able to run further, allowing your breathing to come and go with ease. If your head is squished into your chest, like you see some runners do, you're not releasing as much carbon dioxide as you should be, causing your breathing to become more difficult. When your head is lifted and looking straight forward, your airways for breathing are in an optimal position.

Chest

Your body should be slightly leaned forward with any momentum leaning into the forward traveling motion. Your breath should be a deep breath in and a deep breath out all the while running anywhere from 10 - 14 steps or 5-7 strides.

Back

Keep your back straight and upright. Your shoulders should be slightly pressed backwards and relaxed. Don't straighten your back to the extent that it is a plank, which feeds tension.

No Nos

If you notice you have a bounce in your step, you need to have someone record you so that you can watch yourself running. The more bounce in your step, the more impact you will create for the landing foot after takeoff. It's a good idea to watch elite runners in the front of the pack run a race. You will notice that most of their running almost looks like they're gliding. Their feet are extremely close to the ground, and their bodies don't bounce up and down with each stride. If you tend to bounce when you run you are running at a disadvantage, especially during longer runs. Your body and energy will wear out faster than someone that runs with minimal vertical oscillation (bounce in your step).

Action Steps

- Head up.

- Chest out, with your body leaning slightly forward.

- Back straight.

- Arms should swing naturally, not above the belly button.

- Relax your shoulders.

- Your feet should land over your hip not out in front.

- Don't over-stride.

- Don't bounce while running.

Chapter 5

Warming Up & Cooling Down

Warming Up

Warming up for a 10K should take less than 10 minutes. You do not want to do static stretching before running, unless you are stiff or sore. If you are sore, this may be caused by not properly stretching after your last run. Your 10K training will involve longer and longer runs. After these longer runs you need to make sure that you are stretching adequately especially the quads, hips, calfs, and hamstrings. Also, if you continue to be sore after your runs this could be a sign that you have the wrong shoes. The location of the soreness could else give you a clue. For example, if your feet are sore have a look at your socks and shoes. I'm not saying that you should never be sore after running, however you shouldn't be sore consistently after every run. Remember to use a foam roller as part of your cool down routine to help alleviate soreness and stiffness.

Dynamic stretches can include:

- Leg swings
- Walking knee raises
- Walking lunges
- Light jogging

Cooling Down

Proper cooling down and stretching is equally important as warming up. I use the following cool down guidelines. These are minimum distances that I walk after my runs. Most of the time I will walk two miles after each run so that I can unwind my legs and stretch.

Distance Ran	Cooldown (miles)
1-3	0.5
4-6	1
7-9	1.25
10-12	1.5

When performing static stretching you want to hold and release. Do not bounce while holding the stretch. Hold the stretch anywhere from 20 seconds to 2 minutes. Stretch and use your foam roller to help with soreness.

Static stretches can include:

- Standing quad
- Standing calf
- Hip revolutions
- Wall calf
- Bent hamstring

Rest

Adequate rest is needed just as much as your actual running hours and miles for training. As your running body continues to push itself into longer runs, your rest becomes even more important. In order for your glycogen stores to be refilled properly your body needs to take time off from running or hard physical exertion. After your runs, your body needs time to rebuild and repair the damage taken during your runs. It takes your legs up to 24 hours after each run over 2 miles to repair. Your body continues to build your muscles during the remainder of the week's runs. Depending on your age, you should be getting an adequate amount of sleep each night. On average the human adult needs anywhere from 7 to 8 hours of sleep. During your training, you need to shoot for getting at least 7 hours of sleep a night.

If you choose to drink alcohol, try not to drink alcohol the night before your long run. Also, don't drink alcohol the night of your long run. If you want to have a couple beers, drinks, or glasses of wine, I totally get it. Try not to drink more than two servings and try to drink them at least two hours before bedtime. When you excessively drink alcohol prior to going to bed for the night, the alcohol causes restlessness in sleep which leads to your body not rebuilding with 100% efficiency.

Your mind and body need to enter into a deep sleep cycles for optimal body repairs. Alcohol has been shown to interrupt these cycles preventing your body from accessing deeper sleep.

Action Steps

- Before you run only perform dynamic stretching unless you are still sore after performing the stretches.
- Post-run you will want to perform several hold and release static stretches to help your body recover.
- Get adequate rest during your training cycle.

Chapter 6

Eat Like a Runner

Pre-Run

Before your runs, you will need to get into the habit of trying to eat at least two hours before your run. If you eat a burrito and then immediately attempt to run for thirty minutes, your body might disagree with your decision.

Your pre-run fuel should involve some carbohydrate such as a couple of pieces of bread or an energy bar. Sip on water but avoid the temptation to guzzle 12 ounces right before you run.

Post-Run

After your runs replenish your body with something light like a banana, an apple, or a light protein shake. Drink water and avoid drinking Gatorade altogether. Gatorade serves a purpose, but it's not vital for short distance races unless you lose a lot of fluid through sweating. A sodium and electrolyte replacement is needed when you run longer races such as half marathons because your body sweats out more sodium.

Losing Weight

If one of the other primary reasons for running a 10K is to

lose weight, then you need to pay close attention to the following. Nothing has changed in the scientific community about losing weight and gaining weight. Your body, on a daily basis, needs between 2000 and 2500 calories a day to maintain your current weight. Having said that you would be surprised at how many new runners will run 1 or 2 miles and then consume a double cheeseburger with a side order of fries. Weight loss doesn't work this way. Let's breakdown two examples:

To lose one pound of weight you have to burn 3,500 calories. The only way to increase the rate at which you burn calories, without artificial supplements, is to either consume fewer calories or burn more calories. Thankfully, there are tons of apps on the market that will help you achieve this. Living Strong, My Fitness Pal, Lose it!, and many others.

Example #1 - Gaining Weight

Sally's recommended daily caloric intake is around 2300 calories. All of her meals for the day equal 3,300 calories. She manages to run 3 miles for the day, which burns about 167 calories a mile. Her total caloric surplus would be 500 calories.

+ 3,300 calories consumed

- 2,300 calorie budget

-    500 calories burnt running

_____

+500 calories surplus (a marginal weight **gain**)

If she continues this daily eating pattern each day for one week she will have have **gained roughly 1 pound** (500 calories * 7 days = 3,500 calories. To lose 1 pound of body weight you have to burn 3,500 calories.) If you add these values up over a month or a year, you can easily see how we slowly gain weight in small increments. From the example above, let's look at the outcast for an entire year if you decided to follow this diet plan:

52 weeks * 1 pound/week = 52 pounds in 1 year. Sally would gain 52 pounds in 1 year.

By simply tracking how much you eat in a day could be the one key element you're missing from preventing you from losing weight.

Example #2 - Losing Weight

Susan's recommended daily caloric intake is around 2000 calories. All of her meals for the day equal 2,450 calories. She manages to run 3 miles for the day, which burns about 133 calories a mile. Her total caloric deficit would be 250 calories.

+ 2,150 calories consumed

- 2,000 calorie budget

-    400 calories burnt running

_____

-250 calories deficit (a marginal weight **loss**)

If she continues this daily eating pattern each day for one week, she will have **lost roughly a 1/2 a pound** (250 calorie deficit * 7 days = 1,750 calories. To lose 1 pound of body weight you have to burn 3,500 calories.) If you add these values up over a month or a year, you can easily see how we can slowly lose weight in small increments. From the example above, let's look at the outcast for an entire year if you decided to follow this diet plan:

52 weeks * - 0.5 pounds/week = - 26 pounds in 1 year. Susan would lose 26 pounds over the course of a year.

By simply tracking how much you eat in a day you can visually see how many calories you need to work with and how much is left towards the end of the day. Tracking your food intake could be the one key element you're missing from preventing you from losing weight. Looking at the example on paper is much easier than following the actual habit of sticking to this diet plan for an entire year. If it were easy we could simply eat the same meals for breakfast, lunch, and dinner but most of us can't sustain that time of rigid diet plan. By knowing how much you have eaten you can still indulge in foods you wish to eat as long as the foods caloric count is within your calorie budget for the day. If you track your eating habits with an application, you will be able to stick with the habit of eating less for a much longer length of time. There are lots of free calorie trackers on the market. My two favorite calorie trackers are *Lose It!* and *My Fitness Pal.*

Action Steps

- Pre-run - eat light carbs such as bread or a protein bar.

- Post-run - eat some fruit or a protein shake.

- To lose weight you must consume fewer calories than your daily caloric budget, burn more calories, or a combination of the two.

Chapter 7

Pace Prediction

10K Pace Predictor

To determine your 10k predicted pace, multiply your 5K pace by 2.077. This will give you an estimated predicated finish time which you can then use to calculate how fast your pace per mile should be. If you've only run one 5K race, then just use that time. If you've run multiple 5Ks within a years' time, calculate the average 5K finish time by adding up all your 5K race times and divided by the total number of 5K races.

10K Pace Predictor Example 1

Example 1: Juan has run multiple 5Ks within about 6 months of each other. Here are his race results:

5K race #1: 29:43

5K race #2: 31:24

5K race #3: 29:10

5K race #4: 33:15

Average 5K finish time: 30:53

10K predicted finish time:

30:53 * 2.077 (prediction factor)

30 minutes

53 seconds/60 seconds = 0.88

30.88 * 2.077 (prediction factor) = 64.14

64.14 minutes / 60 minutes = 1.069 hours

Convert back into hours/minutes/seconds:

0.069 * 60 seconds = 4 minutes 0.14 seconds

0.14 seconds * 60 seconds = 8 seconds

1 hour + 4 minutes + 8 seconds = **<u>1:04:08</u> 10K predicted finish time**

10K Pace Predictor Example 2

Example 2: Mary has only run one 5K. Her result was:

5k Race: 35:00

35:00 * 2.077 (prediction factor)

35 minutes

35.00 * 2.077 (prediction factor) = 72.70

72.70 minutes / 60 minutes = 1.21 hours

Convert back into hours/minutes/seconds:

0.21 * 60 seconds = 12 minutes 0.6 seconds

0.6 seconds * 60 seconds = 36 seconds

1 hour + 12 minutes + 36 seconds = **1:12:36 10k**
predicted finish time.

10K Pace Predictor Table

5K Finish Time	10K Predicted Finish Time
0:25	0:52
0:26	0:54
0:27	0:56
0:28	0:58
0:29	1:00
0:30	1:02
0:31	1:04
0:32	1:06
0:33	1:09
0:34	1:11
0:35	1:13
0:36	1:15
0:37	1:17
0:38	1:19
0:39	1:21
0:40	1:23
0:41	1:25
0:42	1:27

0:43	1:29
0:44	1:31
0:45	1:33
0:46	1:36
0:47	1:38
0:48	1:40
0:49	1:42
0:50	1:44

It's only a prediction

When you're calculating your pace, prediction remember that it's only an estimate. Don't get mentally stuck thinking that you will run the exact 10K pace prediction. More than likely you will run faster than your estimated finish time because of the excitement of the race and the adrenaline pumping through your blood. Simply use the pace prediction to help you target an attainable finish time during training. When it comes to race day shoot for the moon and beat your 10K pace prediction.

Chapter 8

Beginner Training Schedule

Six Week Training Schedule

If you can currently run a 5K then you can be trained in 4 weeks to run the distance of a 10K. If you need a little bit of time to get back into your running groove, then it will take you about 6 weeks of training to be ready for a 10K.

IMPORTANT!

If you're having trouble completing a 5k or your brand new to running, I highly suggest you start with an extremely conservative training program such as one I have designed. By following a more conservative and easier paced training program, you will increase the odds of sticking with running for a longer time. My book, *5K Fury*, can guide you through a step-by-step approach by using a run/walk technique. The 5K training takes up to nine weeks and can be finished sooner depending on how physically fit you are. *5K Fury,* is book number 2 in the series, Beginner to Finisher. This is FREE to read with Kindle Unlimited. After you've completed the training for the 5K you can transition into the 4-6-week 10K training program.

—>   **Click here to read 5K Fury**   <—

Differences Between the 5K and 10K

Obviously, one difference between a 5K and a 10K is the distance. A 5K is equivalent to the distance of 3.1 miles. A 10K doubles that distances to 6.2 miles. Another big difference is the approach you take to training for a 10K. While some runners don't need to train at all for 10Ks, most new and intermediate runners need to allow 4 to 6 weeks to be able to adequately run the distance of a 10K.

If you've raced in 5K event where a 10K event takes place as well, you might have noticed the total amount of participants for a 10K is much smaller than a 5K. Why are there fewer participants for the 10K rather than the 5K? That's an easy question to answer, right? Either, "It's harder," or "it's longer," probably popped into your head. While training for a 10K is harder and does require more time to train, it can still be easily accomplished if you schedule your training time and show up for training each week. It's time to hold yourself accountable for your actions. No more excuses.

Long Duration Run

In both of my other books, *5k Fury* and *Beginner's Guide to Half Marathons,* I offer only one training schedule per book.

For most first time 5K runners and half marathon runners, the primary goal is to simply finish the race. A 10K race is slightly different in that many runners come straight from running 5Ks and dive into 10Ks. Some of the participants are already seasoned and just need a small push into the next level of running. The following two schedules, beginner and advanced, are different in how fast you push yourself into the long-distance run. The long distance run or, long duration run, is any run above 3.1 miles. Other sources label a long distance run as anything greater than 5 miles. For simplicity sake when I refer to a long distance run it's any distance greater than 3.1 miles (5K).

How can runners run for that great of a distance? Training is the answer.

Why do some runners progress beyond the 5K and others don't? I believe that there are many reasons why. Some runners don't make the leap due to the simple fact that they have absolutely zero desire to run anything beyond the distance of a 5K. There is absolutely nothing wrong with running 5Ks the rest of your life and never progressing beyond that level. The 5K race acts as a gateway race that leads some runners to push beyond the 5K. One of the main reasons, I believe, is that they simply don't have someone pushing them to the next level. A second reason for not pushing beyond 5Ks is mental blocks. Runners think that 10Ks are for experienced runners. Putting doubt in one's abilities leads to not moving to the next step. The believe that has propelled myself through most of my running is if I can run a 5K then I can run a marathon. All the seasoned runners running half marathons once a month and multi marathons a year all had to begin somewhere. The difference between someone who chooses to run a 10K and someone that doesn't is the belief and drive that they can do it. All experienced runners went through the beginning stages of learning how to run and train. While you can argue that some veteran runners started running in their youth ages, each year many new runners in their thirties and older start running careers. If your body is physically fit to sustain endurance running, you can start running at any age.

Beginner Training Schedule

The beginner training schedule is best suited for runners that have been running for less than one year and can complete a 5K distance (3.1 miles). The total time required to train at the beginner level is six weeks. If you begin training with the beginner's training schedule and you find it too easy, you may want to switch to the advanced training schedule. The advanced training schedule takes only four weeks to complete. If you begin training with the beginner's training schedule and find it too difficult, you may want to ease off for a week and restart training at the 5k level. I offer an easy to follow nine-week 5K training schedule that uses a run/walk technique to get you to the finish line. The book and training schedule can be found in my book, *5K Fury*.

10K Beginner Training Schedule

Week #	Mon.	Tues. (EP)	Wed. (10KP)	Thur. (MP)	Fri.	Sat. (LD)	Sun.
1	Rest	2 mi	2 mi	2 mi	Rest	2.5 mi	Rest/CT
2	Rest	2mi	3 mi	2 mi	Rest	3 mi	Rest/CT
3	Rest	2.5 mi	3 mi	2.5 mi	Rest	3.5 mi	Rest/CT
4	Rest	3 mi	3 mi	2 mi	Rest	4.0 mi	Rest/CT
5	Rest	3 mi	4 mi	2 mi	Rest	4.5 mi	Rest/CT
6	Rest	3 mi	2 mi	Rest	Rest	10K	Rest/CT

(Easy)
EP=Easy Pace, 10KP=Predicted Pace,
MP=Medium Pace, LD=Long Duration, CT=Cross Train

A summarized training schedule and log sheet can be downloaded below for FREE:

CLICK BELOW ON LINK:

FREE 10K training schedule and log sheet

Beginner Training - Week 1

Monday	**Rest.** Take it easy. Don't run. If you need to exercise, I recommend a walk for no longer than 30 minutes.
Tuesday	**Run 2 miles at an easy pace. If you can hold a conversation with someone else you are running at an easy pace, the easy pace is anywhere from 30 seconds to about 1 minute slower than your 10K predicted pace.**
Wednesday	**Run 2 miles at your 10K predicted pace. You should be able to keep up with your 10K predicted pace without becoming winded. If you become winded slow down to a brisk walk for a few minutes and then try to complete your mileage for the day.**
Thursday	**Run 2 miles at an easy pace. The easy pace is anywhere from 30 seconds to about 1 minute slower than your 10K predicted pace.**
Friday	**Rest.** For your muscles to grow stronger, they need rest. Feel free to walk for a few miles. Your Saturday runs are your long duration runs.
Saturday	**Run 2.5 miles at an easy pace.**
Sunday	**Rest.** For beginner runners, this day needs to be kept at a mild rest day. If your body feels good, then go ahead and do cross training for 30 to 60 minutes.

Beginner Training - Week 2

Monday	**Rest.** Take it easy. Don't run. If you need to exercise, I recommend a walk for no longer than 30 minutes.
Tuesday	**Run 2 miles at an easy pace. If you can hold a conversation with someone else you are running at an easy pace, the easy pace is anywhere from 30 seconds to about 1 minute slower than your 10K predicted pace.**
Wednesday	**Run 3 miles at your 10K predicted pace. You should be able to keep up with your 10K predicted pace without becoming winded. If you become winded slow down to a brisk walk for a few minutes and then try to complete your mileage for the day.**
Thursday	**Run 2 miles at an easy pace. The easy pace is anywhere from 30 seconds to about 1 minute slower than your 10K predicted pace.**
Friday	**Rest.** For your muscles to grow stronger, they need rest. Feel free to walk for a few miles. Your Saturday runs are your long duration runs.
Saturday	**Run 3.0 miles at an easy pace.**
Sunday	**Rest.** For beginner runners, this day needs to be kept at a mild rest day. If your body feels good, then go ahead and do cross training for 30 to 60 minutes.

Monday	**Rest.** Take it easy. Don't run. If you need to exercise, I recommend a walk for no longer than 30 minutes.
Tuesday	**Run 2.5 miles at an easy pace. If you can hold a conversation with someone else you are running at an easy pace, the easy pace is anywhere from 30 seconds to about 1 minute slower than your 10K predicted pace.**
Wednesday	**Run 3 miles at your 10K predicted pace. You should be able to keep up with your 10K predicted pace without becoming winded. If you become winded slow down to a brisk walk for a few minutes and then try to complete your mileage for the day.**
Thursday	**Run 2.5 miles at an easy pace. The easy pace is anywhere from 30 seconds to about 1 minute slower than your 10K predicted pace.**
Friday	**Rest.** For your muscles to grow stronger, they need rest. Feel free to walk for a few miles. Your Saturday runs are your long duration runs.
Saturday	**Run 3.5 miles at an easy pace.**
Sunday	**Rest.** For beginner runners, this day needs to be kept at a mild rest day. If your body feels good, then go ahead and do cross training for 30 to 60 minutes.

Beginner Training - Week 4

Monday	**Rest.** Take it easy. Don't run. If you need to exercise, I recommend a walk for no longer than 30 minutes.
Tuesday	**Run 3 miles at an easy pace. If you can hold a conversation with someone else you are running at an easy pace, the easy pace is anywhere from 30 seconds to about 1 minute slower than your 10K predicted pace.**
Wednesday	**Run 3 miles at your 10K predicted pace. You should be able to keep up with your 10K predicted pace without becoming winded. If you become winded slow down to a brisk walk for a few minutes and then try to complete your mileage for the day.**
Thursday	**Run 2 miles at an easy pace. The easy pace is anywhere from 30 seconds to about 1 minute slower than your 10K predicted pace.**
Friday	**Rest.** For your muscles to grow stronger, they need rest. Feel free to walk for a few miles. Your Saturday runs are your long duration runs.
Saturday	**Run 4.0 miles at an easy pace.**
Sunday	**Rest.** For beginner runners, this day needs to be kept at a mild rest day. If your body feels good, then go ahead and do cross training for 30 to 60 minutes.

Beginner Training - Week 5

Monday	Rest. Take it easy. Don't run. If you need to exercise, I recommend a walk for no longer than 30 minutes.
Tuesday	**Run 3 miles at an easy pace. If you can hold a conversation with someone else you are running at an easy pace, the easy pace is anywhere from 30 seconds to about 1 minute slower than your 10K predicted pace.**
Wednesday	**Run 4 miles at your 10K predicted pace. You should be able to keep up with your 10K predicted pace without becoming winded. If you become winded slow down to a brisk walk for a few minutes and then try to complete your mileage for the day.**
Thursday	**Run 2 miles at an easy pace. The easy pace is anywhere from 30 seconds to about 1 minute slower than your 10K predicted pace.**
Friday	**Rest.** For your muscles to grow stronger, they need rest. Feel free to walk for a few miles. Your Saturday runs are your long duration runs.
Saturday	**Run 4.5 miles at an easy pace.**
Sunday	**Rest.** For beginner runners, this day needs to be kept at a mild rest day. If your body feels good, then go ahead and do cross training for 30 to 60 minutes.

Beginner Training - Week 6

Monday	**Rest.** Take it easy. Don't run. If you need to exercise, I recommend a walk for no longer than 30 minutes.
Tuesday	<u>**Run 3 miles at an easy pace.**</u> **If you can hold a conversation with someone else you are running at an easy pace, the easy pace is anywhere from 30 seconds to about 1 minute slower than your 10K predicted pace.**
Wednesday	<u>**Run 2 miles at your 10K predicted pace.**</u> **You should be able to keep up with your 10K predicted pace without becoming winded. If you become winded slow down to a brisk walk for a few minutes and then try to complete your mileage for the day.**
Thursday	**Rest.** Race day in two days. Do not run.
Friday	**Rest.** Race day in one day. Do not run.
Saturday	******* 10K Race. *******
Sunday	**Rest.**

Chapter 9

Advanced Training Schedule

Advanced Training Schedule

The advanced training schedule is best suited for runners that have been running for more than six months and can complete a 5K distance (3.1 miles). The total time required to train at the advanced training level is four weeks. If you begin training with the advanced training schedule and you find it too difficult, you may want to switch to the beginner training schedule. If you begin training with the beginner's training schedule and find that too difficult, you may want to start with the basic 5K training until your body is sustaining one and two mile runs. My book, *5K Fury,* offers an easy to follow nine-week 5K training schedule that uses a run/walk technique to get you to the finish line. The book and training schedule can be found in my book, *5K Fury.*

Table 2 - Advanced Schedule

10K Advanced Training Schedule

Week #	Mon.	Tues. (EP)	Wed. (10KP)	Thur. (MP)	Fri.	Sat. (LD)	Sun.
1	Rest	3 mi	3 mi	3 mi	Rest	3 mi	Rest/CT
2	Rest	3 mi	3.5 mi	3 mi	Rest	4 mi	Rest/CT
3	Rest	3 mi	4 mi	2 mi	Rest	5 mi	Rest/CT
4	Rest	3 mi	2 mi	Rest	Rest	10K	Rest/CT

(Advanced)
EP=Easy Pace, 10KP=Predicted Pace,
MP=Medium Pace, LD=Long Duration, CT=Cross Train

A summarized training schedule and log sheet can be downloaded below for FREE:

CLICK BELOW ON LINK:

FREE 10K training schedule and log sheet

Monday	**Rest.** Take it easy. Don't run. If you need to exercise, I recommend a walk for no longer than 30 minutes.
Tuesday	**Run 3 miles at an easy pace. If you can hold a conversation with someone else you are running at an easy pace, the easy pace is anywhere from 30 seconds to about 1 minute slower than your 10K predicted pace.**
Wednesday	**Run 3 miles at your 10K predicted pace. You should be able to keep up with your 10K predicted pace without becoming winded. If you become winded slow down to a brisk walk for a few minutes and then try to complete your mileage for the day.**
Thursday	**Run 3 miles at an easy pace. The easy pace is anywhere from 30 seconds to about 1 minute slower than your 10K predicted pace.**
Friday	**Rest.** For your muscles to grow stronger, they need rest. Feel free to walk for a few miles. Your Saturday runs are your long duration runs.
Saturday	**Run 3.0 miles at an easy pace.**
Sunday	**Rest.** For beginner runners, this day needs to be kept at a mild rest day. If your body feels good, then go ahead and do some form of cross training for 30 to 60 minutes.

Advanced Training - Week 2

Monday	**Rest.** Take it easy. Don't run. If you need to exercise, I recommend a walk for no longer than 30 minutes.
Tuesday	<u>**Run 3 miles at an easy pace.**</u> **If you can hold a conversation with someone else you are running at an easy pace, the easy pace is anywhere from 30 seconds to about 1 minute slower than your 10K predicted pace.**
Wednesday	<u>**Run 3.5 miles at your 10K predicted pace.**</u> **You should be able to keep up with your 10K predicted pace without becoming winded. If you become winded slow down to a brisk walk for a few minutes and then try to complete your mileage for the day.**
Thursday	<u>**Run 3 miles at an easy pace.**</u> **The easy pace is anywhere from 30 seconds to about 1 minute slower than your 10K predicted pace.**
Friday	**Rest.** For your muscles to grow stronger, they need rest. Feel free to walk for a few miles. Your Saturday runs are your long duration runs.
Saturday	<u>**Run 4.0 miles at an easy pace.**</u>
Sunday	**Rest.** For beginner runners, this day needs to be kept at a mild rest day. If your body feels good, then go ahead and do cross training for 30 to 60 minutes.

Advanced Training - Week 3

Monday	**Rest.** Take it easy. Don't run. If you need to exercise, I recommend a walk for no longer than 30 minutes.
Tuesday	**Run 3 miles at an easy pace. If you can hold a conversation with someone else you are running at an easy pace, the easy pace is anywhere from 30 seconds to about 1 minute slower than your 10K predicted pace.**
Wednesday	**Run 4 miles at your 10K predicted pace. You should be able to keep up with your 10K predicted pace without becoming winded. If you become winded slow down to a brisk walk for a few minutes and then try to complete your mileage for the day.**
Thursday	**Run 2 miles at an easy pace. The easy pace is anywhere from 30 seconds to about 1 minute slower than your 10K predicted pace.**
Friday	**Rest.** For your muscles to grow stronger, they need rest. Feel free to walk for a few miles. Your Saturday runs are your long duration runs.
Saturday	**Run 5.0 miles at an easy pace.**
Sunday	**Rest.** For beginner runners, this day needs to be kept at a mild rest day. If your body feels good, then go ahead and cross training for 30 to 60 minutes.

Advanced Training - Week 4

Monday	**Rest.** Take it easy. Don't run. If you need to exercise, I recommend a walk for no longer than 30 minutes.
Tuesday	**<u>Run 3 miles at an easy pace</u>. If you can hold a conversation with someone else you are running at an easy pace, the easy pace is anywhere from 30 seconds to about 1 minute slower than your 10K predicted pace.**
Wednesday	**<u>Run 2 miles at your 10K predicted pace</u>. You should be able to keep up with your 10K predicted pace without becoming winded. If you become winded slow down to a brisk walk for a few minutes and then try to complete your mileage for the day.**
Thursday	**Rest.** Race day in two days. Do not run.
Friday	**Rest.** Race day in one day. Do not run.
Saturday	***** 10K Race. *****
Sunday	**Rest.**

Action Steps

- Stick to your training schedule.

- If you can't run on a given day, change your schedule and don't worry about it.

- Continue walking for at least 10 minutes after a running session.

- Cross training will help you stay active on your non-running days.

- A 30 to 60-minute walk is an excellent source of cross training.

Chapter 10

Relax the Day Before the Race

Night Before the Race

A lot of people will find it difficult to get enough sleep the night before your first 10K. Some runners will run a few light miles the day before the race. Lay out your running gear so that it will be ready in the morning. This gear includes your clothing, tech gear, waters, gels, hydration packs, water bottles, running shoes, bib, sunglasses, sunblock, headband, and socks. If you picked up your racing runner's packet early, go ahead and pin the racing number on your shirt or shorts. Do not drink alcohol. Your body needs to be as hydrated as possible.

Action Steps

- Get all your gear laid out, including clothes, water, phone, phone case Garmins, and Fitbits.

- Attach your bib number to your clothes.

- Know what route you are going to take to the race.

- Keep hydrating.

- Your last dinner before the race shouldn't be a big meal.

- Get at least 7 hours of sleep (might be hard to do this because of anxiety).

- If you are getting edgy or antsy, go for a mile or two walk.

Chapter 11

Get Pumped - It's Race Day

Race Day

The day has finally arrived. Wake up a couple of hours early before the race start time. Eat a small meal as soon as possible. This meal should have some carbohydrates, such as a bagel or toast with peanut butter, maybe a few eggs, and water. This meal should be anywhere from 400 to 600 calories. Avoid high fiber content food. Drink a cup of coffee if you like. Drink about 12 oz of water before the race. Continue to sip on water leading up to the race. Remember you don't want a sloshing stomach, so don't over drink.

When runners begin to line up for the race, you need to pick the correct starting location in the herd. Do not line up at the front of the starting line unless you are going to run the 10K fast! If you're not planning on running the 10K fast, you probably need to be somewhere in the middle. You could easily get stampeded or hurt someone else if you attempt to be in the front of the line and not race fast. The slowest paced runners such as the walkers need to be in the back of the queue. The average paced runners should be located in the middle of the herd, roughly between the first 20% and 60% of racers. I have, on many races, thought I was in the correct location somewhere in the middle, and I was wrong. I had to pass many people performing slot type racing just to get out of the muck. The racers at the tail end are more than likely walking or running at a much slower pace. During the race if you need to slow down your pace, you need to move to the right of the course.

Make sure to take it easy out of the gate. Race like you've trained to run the race. Conserve your energy for the first 5 miles. Steady and even pacing just like your training will get you to the finish line. If you have some extra energy towards the end of your 10K (beginning of mile 5), then go ahead and let loose. You will notice that your pace per mile will be faster than your training pace. The excitement, adrenaline and competitive aspects of the race naturally add to the energy surging through your body. So, take it slow at first and run at the pace you've trained at over the last four to six weeks.

Action Steps

Race day:

- Wake up two hours before your race.

- Eat as soon as you get up. Oatmeal, energy bars, and a banana are great sources of food.

- Drink some caffeine about 1-2 hours before the race.

- Keep sipping on water up until race time.

- Don't consume too much water. If your stomach is sloshing around, you drank too much - try to use the restroom.

- Arrive at the race a little early if possible just in case of traffic.

The Race:

- Race like you've trained.

- Remember you don't have to run the entire race. If you get tired slow down to a brisk walk at the water/aid stations for 1/10 mile or 2 minutes, then speed back up.

Chapter 12

Unwind After the Race

Post-Race

Your body will be tired after your 10K race. Admire your new shiny 10K medal. Don't sit down or stop moving all together. Just like during your training after you complete your long runs you need to let your body move into a cool down mode. At a bare minimum keep walking for another 5-10 minutes. If your body feels like it, jog at a light pace for another 2-5 minutes. Grab something to drink with electrolytes if possible. You need to eat something within one hour of completing your race, to help replenish your fluids and give your body nutrients.

If you're up for it, you can drink a beer. Drink plenty of water and keep yourself hydrated over the next couple of days. Sometimes a recovery run the day following your race will help stretch out some of your sore leg muscles. Your recovery run should be at a light pace and not last more than twenty to thirty minutes.

I would avoid normal running for at least 2-3 days to let your legs recover. You should be walking every day after your race. Remember to stretch out your sore muscles after your walks and use your foam roller for extra sore muscles.

Action Steps

Post-Race:

- Don't stop moving at the finish line.

- Keep walking for 10 to 20 minutes after the race.

- Grab a sports drink and some food such as a banana, yogurt, or bread.

- Pose for pictures and enjoy your new, shiny medal.

- Stretch your muscles accordingly.

- Don't run for at least 2-3 days.

Chapter 13
Conclusion

Congratulations

Pat yourself on the back if you have completed your first 10K. No matter how long it took you to finish your race, remember that you did something awesome today while other people sat on the couch. Congratulations!

Pains and Tweaks

Pains that make you want to stop running. These are different than the minor aches and stiffness you get during your run. Many runs I had to stop and just stretch out to alleviate the stiffness. In fact, my muscles aren't fully warmed up until mile number 2. I have yet to have pains that completely stop my running.

As with any physical activity, no two people are exactly alike. The information provided is an example and a guideline, not an absolute rule that you must follow. Adapt anything to your style to suit your needs as a runner. The two biggest running tips of advice given to me were run naturally and breathe deep. These tips helped me through the long duration runs that can take real effort to complete.

Help an Author Out

Thanks for reading! If you've enjoyed this book, please leave me a short, gleaming review on Amazon. If you're having trouble leaving a review just select one thing you liked about the book. I take the time to read every review so that I can change and update this book based on reviewer feedback.

Click here to review book

If you've just finished your first 10K race and you want someone to tell, send me an email. I would be delighted to hear from you.

Follow me on Facebook and Twitter:

Twitter: @BeginR2FinishR

Facebook: facebook.com/BeginnerToFinisher/

Website: www.halfmarathonforbeginners.com

Email: scottmorton@halfmarathonforbeginners.com

What's Next?

If you want to continue your running career, I urge you to either try to beat your personal best 10Ks or start training for a half marathon. If you have used the training schedules provided in this book, then you should only have to train 6 weeks more to prepare yourself for a half marathon. I have full faith that if you crossed the 10K finish line, you could move onto conquering another goal such as a half marathon. If you're feeling super ambitious, you can launch into a half marathon training plan. In my #1 Amazon Best Seller Book, *Beginner's Guide to Half Marathons*, a 12-week training plan will step you through the mental and physical challenges that come with half marathon training. You can read this book for FREE with Kindle Unlimited.

Click here to read now.

For a special sneak peek of,
Why New Runners Fail: 26 Ultimate Tips You Should Know Before You Start Running,
(Book #1 in the Series Beginner to Finisher),
turn to the next page.

Touch here to purchase Ebook version

Touch here to purchase the paperback version

Touch here to purchase the audiobook version

Not Running Enough

Running too little will not allow your body to get used to a training schedule. For example, let's say that you only run two days a week—let's pick Monday and Thursday–to run. Each session consists of 1 mile running followed by 1 mile of walking.

Negatives:

- Your body isn't getting used to running.
- You might be more susceptible to injury because your body isn't able to rebuild and reuse the muscles quickly enough. It's almost like your body is forgetting how to run between workouts.
- You won't be able to progress much further than your training mileage.
- Inadequate running makes the mental struggle harder on the mind. Your mind and body think they are being reset after each run session and are not learning the habit of running.

Positives:

- You are exercising.

I don't think that you should ever drop below an absolute minimum of three days running/walking. I prefer at least four days of running. If you decide to run a maximum of three days, I highly suggest that you skip every other day (see below).

Three days of training

Monday	Tuesday	Wednesday	Thursday	Friday	Saturday	Sunday
Run	Rest	Run	Rest	Run	Rest	Walk

Four days of training (Preferred)

Monday	Tuesday	Wednesday	Thursday	Friday	Saturday	Sunday
Run	Run	Rest	Run	Rest	Run	Walk

Action Steps

- Running too little makes it tougher on your body than having a normal running schedule.
- Don't run less than 3 times a week if you want to progress in the sport of running.

Touch here to purchase Ebook version

Touch here to purchase the paperback version

Touch here to purchase the audiobook version

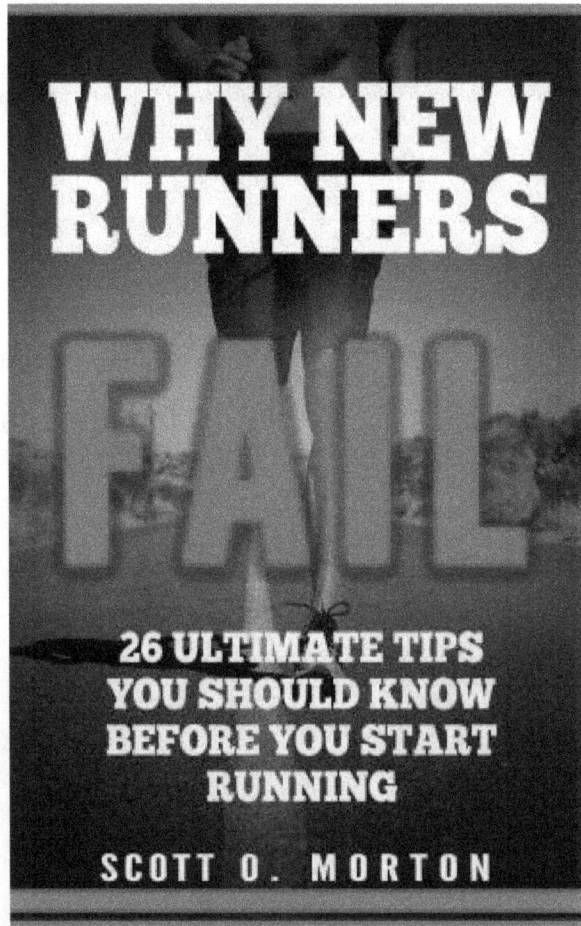

WHY NEW
RUNNERS

FAIL

26 ULTIMATE TIPS
YOU SHOULD KNOW
BEFORE YOU START
RUNNING

SCOTT O. MORTON

For a special sneak peek of,
5K Fury: 10 Proven Steps to Get You to the Finish Line in 9 weeks or less!
(Book #2 in the Series Beginner to Finisher),
turn to the next page.

Touch here to purchase.

Motivation

Why do some people finish marathons and other don't? I believe it comes down to self-motivation and determination. Self-motivation, while probably the strongest of any other form of motivation, is not the only source of motivation. There are several different types of motivation. Three types of motivation that I believe are the most influential come from social media, running partners and yourself.

Social Media

Social media can help keep you focused and motivated by your circle of friends. You can post running times and screen shots of your runs to social media to let your circle of friends comment and cheer you on. Social media will help perk you up when you have a day that you just don't feel like running.

Running Partners

Running partners are the next best thing to yourself keeping you motivated. They train with you. They give you feedback. They help you stay on pace. They push you when you have no more energy. Partners also help you stay accountable for following through with your goal. One caveat to a running partner is that if they lack self-motivation, they aren't going to be of much help motivating you.

Yourself

Self-motivation is by far the most powerful source of motivation. You know yourself better than anyone else. You are custom to knowing how your mind and body work. If you don't feel like running one day, tell yourself that you will just run a half a mile. After you run a half mile, tell yourself that you will just run one mile. By pushing yourself just a little bit, you can trick your mind into running.

Your motivation could be to get healthy and fit. Also, you could be motivated just to prove to yourself that you can finish a 5K or to donate to a worthy cause. Whatever the motivation is, you and only you will finish the race.

Touch here to purchase.

5K Fury: 10 Proven Steps to Get You to the Finish Line in 9 weeks or less!

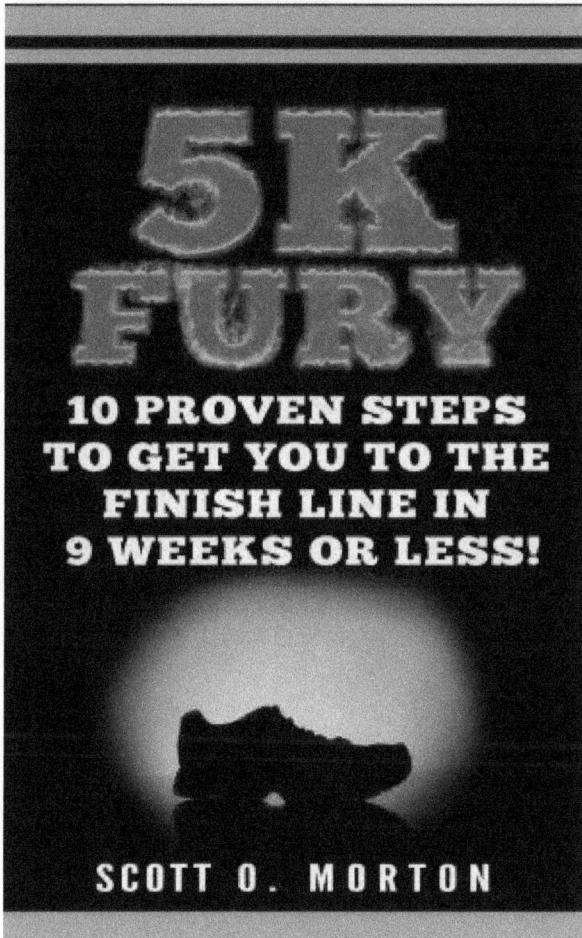

For a special sneak peek of,
10K Titan: Push Beyond the 5K in 6 Weeks or Less!,
(Book #3 in the Series Beginner to Finisher),
turn to the next page.

Touch here to purchase Ebook version

Fear of Running Far

New runners fear running past the distance of a 5K (3.1 miles). Why do we fear running longer distances? Here is a list of some of the reasons we might tell ourselves as to why we don't attempt to run past 3.1 miles:

- I'm not a runner.
- I'm not a long-distance runner.
- I fear that my body might not make it.
- I fear I might get injured.
- There is no way I can run that far and for that long.
- I can't run that far.
- I'm too overweight.
- I'm too out of shape.
- I'm too old.
- People might make fun of me if I tell them I'm training for a 10K.

The list goes well beyond some of the reasons listed above as to why we might be holding ourselves back from running the distance of a 10K. There are too many "I can'ts" above. You have to shake loose the phrase, "I can't." That phrase poisons your mind with disbelief even before you get started.

Touch here to purchase Ebook version

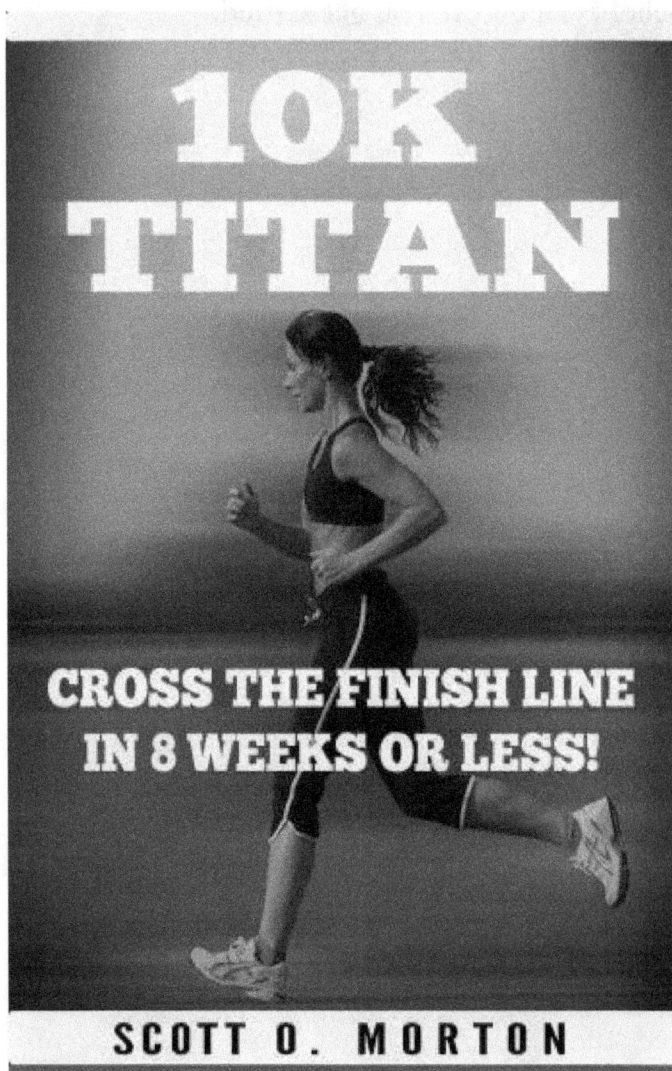

For a special sneak peek of,
Beginner's Guide to Half Marathons: A Simple Step-By-Step Solution to Get You to the Finish Line in 12 Weeks!
(Book #4 in the Series Beginner to Finisher),
turn to the next page.

Beginner's Guide to Half Marathons has become an Amazon #1 Bestseller.

Touch here to purchase eBook version

Touch here to purchase the paperback version

Touch here to purchase the audiobook version

The runner's mindset. Getting past the fear of running 13.1 miles is one of the biggest hurdles of completing a half marathon. I'm going to let you in on a big secret that helped me get past my fear of having to run 13.1 miles. The secret is that most runners don't run the entire 13.1 miles. Wow, what a secret. It's true. The super athletes and other runners trying to beat their personal best records might very well run the entire race. However, I have completed three half marathons and one full marathon, and the majority of runners will walk through the water/aid stations along the course. Once I realized that you don't have to run the entire distance, the fear of running a half marathon vanished, instantly. My mind had found a chink in the armor. Once I exploited the weakness of the 13.1 half marathon beast, my mindset changed forever on long distance running. This same technique allowed me to complete a marathon as well. Someone reading this right now is probably saying, "He's probably been running for a long time." I was able to complete three half marathons and one full marathon over the course of a year. I began in May 2016 and completed my third half marathon on April 22, 2017, at the age of 43 with no prior long distance running experience whatsoever. I'm by no means a super athlete, just an average person with high beliefs that I could finish a half marathon. I hope that this encourages you to finish your first half marathon no matter what age you begin at. If I can do it, so can you.

Finishing a 5K or a 10K can be easily accomplished with little or no training at all. If your goal is to run or walk/run a half marathon, then you must tell yourself that you are a runner. You are no longer running for the sake of exercise. You are running to train your body to complete your first half marathon. You are now training for a half marathon.

Many things that I go over in this book are solely my opinion. Every training schedule discussed within this book has been used by me to complete three half marathons and a full marathon. There are several different schools of thought when it comes to how much running per week it takes to train for a half marathon. There are different nutrition guides, shoe strategies, running miles per week, etc. There is, however, one common thing agreed upon by almost all runners - you have to believe in yourself and believe that you are a runner. Without this firmly ingrained in your head, you won't make it past mile nine, and you won't make it to the finish line. I'm not telling you this to discourage you. I'm telling you this to prepare you for the mental battle of running. One week at a time, one day at a time, one mile at a time, and one step at a time will get you to the half marathon finish line.

Touch here to purchase eBook version

Touch here to purchase the paperback version

Touch here to purchase the audiobook version

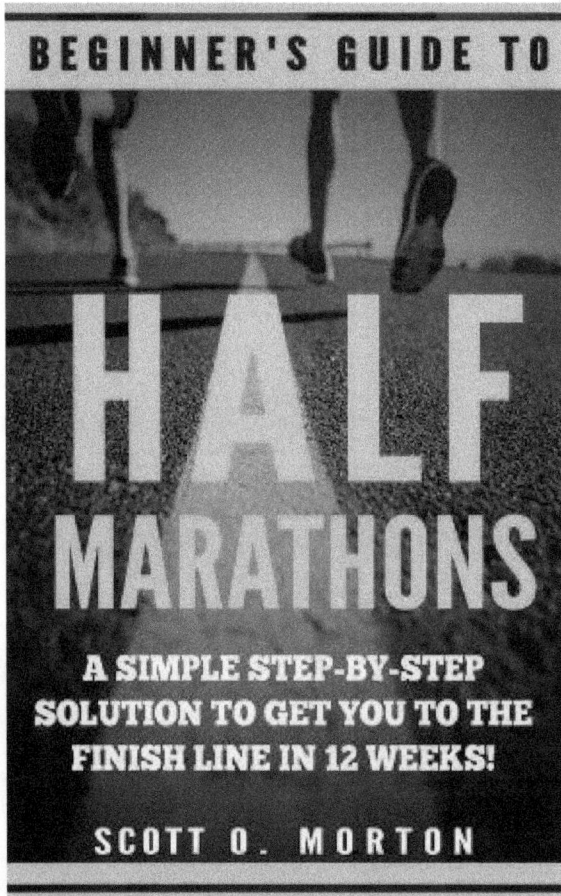

Resources

If you're still unsure of where to start or have other questions regarding running for beginners, please read the first book in the series, Beginner to Finisher Book 1:

CLICK BELOW ON LINK:

Why New Runners Fail: 26 Ultimate Tips You Should Know Before You Start Running!

You can read for FREE with Kindle Unlimited.

A summarized training schedule and log sheet can be downloaded below for FREE:

CLICK BELOW ON LINK:

FREE 10K training schedule and log sheet

About the Author

I played sports throughout my youth and even into my adult years. I ran my first 5k at the age of 37 in March of 2008 without any training at all. I finished third place, although my leg muscles felt like I deserved first place. My legs were sore for six days after the race. My next 5k attempt was in 2015 at the age of 42 in my local hometown. I had no intention of placing at all. I ended up running worse than my first 5k by almost two minutes. I placed second with no training at all. I thought I would have learned a lesson by now - nope.

In May 2016, I was flying to Las Vegas for our yearly guys' trip. I was reading a *Sky Mall* magazine, and I came across an article called "Top 100 things to do in Las Vegas." Number eight on the list was run a race through the streets of Las Vegas. During the race, the city blocks off sections of the strip. I was hooked. They offered a 5k, 10k, half marathon and marathon. I liked walking a lot; in fact, one of my favorite things to do in Las Vegas was to see how many steps I could get in a day (my record to date is 42,000). The Rock-and-Roll Half

Marathon/Marathon would be taking place in November 2016. I scoured the Internet for any information related to training for a half marathon.

My wife asked me, "Why in the world do you want to run a half marathon?" I told her because I was physically able to. She said, "You just want to put one of those 13.1 stickers on the back of your car." But truthfully the real reason was much deeper than that. Whenever I catch a fresh dump of powder on my snowboard, there is no other experience like it. I feel like a kid again, and I feel alive. The real reason I wanted to run was because I wanted to feel the accomplishment, feel the pain and feel the glory of crossing the finish line all the while feeling alive. Running allows me to unleash that competitive kid inside me who yearns to feel alive.

Other Books by Scott Oscar Morton

If you would like to know when I publish my new Ebook releases, please sign up by clicking here. All books can be read for FREE with Kindle Unlimited.

Beginner to Finisher Series:

<u>Available Now:</u>

Book 1: *Why New Runners Fail: 26 Ultimate Tips You Should Know Before You Start Running!*

Book 2: *5K Fury: 10 Proven Steps to Get You to the Finish Line in 9 weeks or less!*

Book 3: *10K Titan: Push Beyond the 5K in 6 Weeks or Less!*

Book 4: *Beginner's Guide to Half Marathons: A Simple Step-By-Step Solution to Get You to the Finish Line in 12 Weeks!*

<u>Coming Soon:</u>

Book 5: *Marathon Motivator: A Simple Step-By-Step Solution to get you to the Finish line in 20 Weeks!*

www.ingramcontent.com/pod-product-compliance
Lightning Source LLC
Chambersburg PA
CBHW031626040426
42452CB00007B/696